GIFT
from Within

GIFTS
from Within

Women's Meditations for Lent

WOMEN OF BRIGID'S PLACE

MOREHOUSE PUBLISHING
Harrisburg, Pennsylvania

Morehouse Publishing
P.O. Box 1321
Harrisburg, PA 17105

Morehouse Publishing is a division of The Morehouse Group.

Cover art by Fiona McGettigan of CORE Design Studio, Houston, Texas

Cover design by Corey Kent

Library of Congress Cataloging-in-Publication Data

Gifts from within : women's meditations for Lent / women of Brigid's Place.
    p. cm.
Includes bibliographical references and index.
    ISBN 0-8192-1895-2 (pbk.)
    1. Lent—Meditations. 2. Women—Religious life. I. Brigid's Place (Houston, Tex.)
    BV85 .G47 2002
    242'.643—dc21

                                                          2002006723

Printed in the United States of America
01 02 03 04 05 06   6 5 4 3 2 1

For

Lois Ann Peckham

1946–1999

whose encouragement and support inspired this book

CONTENTS

ACKNOWLEDGMENTS

Had it not been for the encouragement and support of Lois Ann Peckham, to whom this book is dedicated, we would not have begun the adventure of writing *Gifts from Within*. We would like to extend a special thanks to those who have shared their thoughts and helped to publish our previous meditations: Kaye Bernard, Sandi Glorfield, Madeleine Manning, Judy Mood, Rob Mood, Mary Sieber, Cora Spear, and Patty Turney. Thanks as well to Debra Farrington at Morehouse Publishing, who discovered our meditation article in the *Journal of Women's Ministries* and contacted us to find out more.

INTRODUCTION

Brigid's Place is a nonprofit, ecumenical organization that supports the spiritual development of women. It is a ministry of Christ Church Cathedral, an Episcopal church located in downtown Houston. Women come here for classes, lectures, discussion groups, weekend workshops, and retreats. They ask questions relating to their spiritual journeys, address their doubts, and become empowered to meet the challenges of life. We chose our name in honor of Saint Brigid, a fifth-century Irish saint who founded a monastery of nuns and monks known for their wisdom, compassion, hospitality, and healing. Saint Brigid emphasized the equality of men and women.

At Brigid's Place, we encourage women to share their lives with one another as we build a community where everyone is welcome. Brigid's Place will always be evolving—open to hearing and answering the needs of women in their spiritual development. It was out of this nurturing environment that these Lenten meditations were born.

In mid-November of 1997, the Searching the Scriptures group at Brigid's Place was just ending its weekly study of the Book of John, using commentaries from feminist theologians. One of the members bemoaned the lack of Lenten meditations from a feminist point of view. To her, and to many of us in the group, Lent still seemed to emphasize denial and the diminishment of self instead of providing an opportunity for growth and healing. We asked ourselves: How can we view the life-giving experience of Jesus during this transformational time? As women in our forties and fifties, we no longer wanted to experience any self-contempt for "not being enough." We needed something that was truth telling and real for us. What better way to find it than to do it ourselves?

Time was short, but Lois Ann Peckham and Patty Turney gathered writers, gave them assignments from the daily lectionary, and set deadlines. We did not anticipate some of their complaints: "I don't like my choices of readings." "I'm having trouble writing using these

Scriptures." "This is making me angry and it's difficult to write." We encouraged the contributors to use their anger or frustration as a springboard to their creativity, working through their feelings as they wrote the meditations.

This book contains selections from the 1998 through 2001 issues of our *Women's Lenten Meditations*. As I write this, our 2002 issue has just returned from the printer, continuing our tradition of encouraging women to voice their deepest feelings and experiences. These meditations reflect the struggles of many women as they try to be faithful to the challenge of the Holy Spirit: that is, to be authentic to the people God created them to be—themselves. Writers are both lay and ordained members of various Christian traditions: Episcopal, Methodist, Roman Catholic, Lutheran, Baptist, and Presbyterian.

With these meditations, the women of Brigid's Place invite you to reflect on your life and question your assumptions on your Lenten journey.

Blessing and peace,
Patty Turney
www.brigidsplace.org

Ash Wednesday Week

ASH WEDNESDAY WEEK

Ash Wednesday
Jonah 3:1–4:11

A dialogue between Jonah and today's psalms: "... cut off
my enemies, and destroy all my adversaries."

Psalm 143:12

And the word of God came to me saying, "Get up, go to those
you fear, those who, in your grief and rage, you ask me to punish,
even destroy. Tell them what I have told you. You have another
chance. You have yet another opportunity to be transformed." Against
my better judgment, I gave them God's message. And I heard them say,
"Happy are those whose offense is forgiven, whose harm to another is
overlooked" (Psalm 32:1).

Those arrogant oppressors! They need to be taken down a notch so
that they may never hurt others as they hurt me and mine! Well! They
acted like they had turned around and looked at the world through
God's eyes. They gloated, "Let's enjoy God's presence with thanks, let's
make joyful noise, sing God's praise!" (Psalm 95:2).

Well, it wasn't fair, and was I angry! I went out where I didn't have
to listen to them, and lay down. At least God gave me shade from the
heat. I waited, hoping—and still praying to see God punish those who
had made me and so many others miserable. "Out of the depths I cry
to you, O God. God, hear my voice" (Psalm 130:1).

Then God sent the sun to shine on me and on them. Sent Ruah, the
breath of the Spirit, to all of us, and I was filled with resentment. It was
their turn to be miserable! I didn't want to join their party! Again I
prayed, "Cut off my enemies and destroy all my adversaries, for I am
your servant" (Psalm 143:12)—and they aren't! But God came to sit
with me. "I have called you children, not servants. You forget," God

said, "that you didn't earn my mercy either. I give life to those who are condemned to die," she said. "You, them, all. My child, do not take lightly the correction of God your Mother. Let me steer you from the death that hate brings to your soul. You can't punish them without crippling yourself, for I have carried each of you in my womb and you are connected forever. Don't lose your joy for life!"

> Let this be told for generations to come, so that a people
> yet unborn may praise God. (Psalm 102:18)

MADELEINE MANNING, daughter and heir of generations of strong women, is a freelance writer and liturgist and a spiritual companion. Passionate about justice, fun, food, glowing, and friends, she vows to stop buying books about simplicity, for they are cluttering her ever-evolving home. She is grateful to be living in this time of blossoming awareness of the divine feminine.

Thursday after Ash Wednesday
Mark 3:19b–35

> *A crowd was sitting around him; and they said to him,*
> *"Your mother and your brothers and sisters are outside,*
> *asking for you." And he replied, "Who are my mother and*
> *my brothers?" And looking at those who sat around him,*
> *he said, "Here are my mother and my brothers! Whoever*
> *does the will of God is my brother and sister and mother."*
>
> *Mark 3:32–35*

Because my familial relationships are so important to me, I have envisioned myself as Jesus' sister or his mother standing outside, feeling rejected and worrying about whether Jesus has "gone out of his mind" (Mark 3:21). But he hasn't rejected his family: he has included others in a household so radically loving that a willing spirit, rather than blood or genes, defines membership. Even an institution as dear as our families of origin is merely a human construct. In Jesus' words I hear that even the most binding, precious connections we have as human beings cannot compare with the deep, indissoluble belonging we share in the Spirit. And for those of us for whom there is no joyful memory of parents or siblings, Jesus' message is that we do have a faithful and caring family.

Many socially constructed barriers—those of clannishness, race, creed, socioeconomic class, gender, or sexual identity—have separated us from other members of God's household. We have allowed ourselves to be labeled in ways that keep us from full participation in God's family. When we reach beyond those illusory barriers, we, like Jesus, are sometimes called out of our minds, or we are criticized for ignoring society's castes.

> May God strengthen us with the joy of our full membership,
> our total belonging to ourselves and to each other,
> and enable us to welcome all our sisters and brothers
> in the household of God. Amen.

MARTHA SERPAS, a graduate of Yale Divinity School and the University of Houston's doctoral program in creative writing, teaches writing, religion, and literature at the University of Tampa. She is a poet.

Friday after Ash Wednesday
John 12:9–19

> . . . *they came not only because of Jesus but also to see*
> *Lazarus, whom he had raised from the dead. So the chief*
> *priests planned to put Lazarus to death as well, since it*
> *was on account of him that many of the Jews were desert-*
> *ing and were believing in Jesus.*
>
> *John 12:9–11*

So, Lazarus stumbles out of the tomb with that "four days dead" smell about him. Mary and Martha are overjoyed and his friends, even the ones who criticized Jesus for not keeping him alive in the first place, are amazed at this miracle. Yet, in the midst of joy and miracle, resurrection and love, we have Lazarus fresh from the dead and under the death threat of the chief priests! This part stops me—"What? This man has just been resurrected and now you want to kill him because people's beliefs are changed?" For me, this is where the story becomes real. I know people are resurrected, and what a glorious experience that is; yet, I know that the world does not take kindly to resurrection, to fundamental changes in who a person is and can be.

Think of experiences where change threatens us: watch a teenager and a parent battle it out as one desires independence and the other learns to let go; watch churches separate rather than accept new modes of being; watch society as we struggle to redefine families in the wake of divorce, single parenting, and same-sex unions; watch our nation as we try to understand what it is to be an American in the midst of a global village. Change, coping with resurrections, is scary, hard, and assaults the core beliefs about the way things are or should be.

As Christians, we are called to be a part of resurrection *and* accepting of the change that it brings—to move beyond our comfort level to see new possibilities and to use the teachings of Jesus to entertain new relationships and types of creation. As a young woman, I find this one of the most freeing and affirming parts of our faith. It allows me to make choices about who I am as a female, whom I choose to love, what I put my time, energy, and money into, who constitutes my family, and what I am able to become. My resurrection experience of being made whole may threaten people just as Lazarus stumbling out of the tomb did. Yet it also may lead me into a new relationship, a new way of imaging the world, and at last, into a resurrection of myself. So, when fear and discomfort become apparent, I need to remind myself to look for resurrection and ways to welcome this miracle into my life.

AIMEE ESTEP is a proud parent and youth minister living in Austin, Texas.

Saturday after Ash Wednesday
1 Corinthians 10:14–17; 11:27–32

For just as the loaf of bread is one, so we are all one body;
for we are all partakers of that one bread.
                                              1 Corinthians 10:17

Discovering the body of Christ on a winter's night . . .

November in Connecticut is cold, gray, and always leafless. One plows through winter with steely determination. Often during these bleak times I felt mildly isolated from others, and to combat this I filled my life with purposeful activities. One particular winter I was completing my master's degree in special education in order to help me become more effective in the classroom where I was teaching English.

My graduate class was meeting at the Southern Connecticut Home for the Retarded, where we were to see the facilities and hear more about the residents. We had studied the different stages of mental retardation, teaching strategies, and creative curriculum development, all the tools for "successful teaching." But I was not prepared for the dramatic and life-changing experience this winter evening would bring.

The professor had described the world of the profoundly retarded, but I had not expected to see other human beings so cruelly broken. Some could not speak—only grunt and moan as they lay in beds or partially sat in chairs and cribs. "How can this be?" my well-ordered heart called out. "Can't we do something?" I remembered the words of my professor: "Touch and feel—this is how these people feel contact." As I walked through the residence, I came to a young man partially sitting in a crib of sorts. He must have been in his early twenties, not much older than our two sons, who were at home studying or, more likely, playing basketball. His hand crept slowly toward his shoulder. He must have felt an itch or a pain. He kept reaching, never quite connecting with the pain. Without thinking, I touched him on the shoulder and gently began to rub his back. He slowly turned his head toward me, and as our eyes met, I felt something stir within me. Suddenly I was part of him as he was part of me. In that moment of recognition we were one body, each broken in our own particular ways, but together we were one. Christ called me that night into a new relationship—a new understanding of our oneness. I would never see the disabled, the handicapped, or anyone for that matter, as people to be taught. Each had now become my sister and brother in Christ. Together we were a community of learners.

MARY TAYLOR is a retired educator living in Lenox, Massachusetts, with her husband, Walter, a retired Episcopal priest. They have two married sons and four grandchildren.

First Week
of Lent

FIRST WEEK OF LENT

First Sunday of Lent
Mark 5:21–24, 35–43
Luke 8:40–42, 49–56
Matthew 9:18–19, 23–26

For years, I have run from thinking deeply about my relationship with my father—just as he has fled from me through emotional detachment. I have no memories of overt harm in our relationship. In fact, I have almost no memories of relationship. Though we lived in the same house for eighteen years, my eyes rarely met his.

Reading the story of Jairus's daughter, I wondered what it was like to be her—to be young, sick, and dying at a time when medical experts were nonexistent. I wondered if her illness was sudden, or if her father had sought other help over previous days—solutions that had failed. Or had he delayed approaching Jesus out of fear of repercussions at work? As the synagogue's ruler, probably from Capernaum, it was at best politically risky for him to seek help from this controversial new prophet, Jesus.

Would my dad have gone? If I look honestly at his life, there's evidence for doubting that his love for me and his faith in God would have been stronger than his fear. (Ugh, this is not where I wanted this story to take me.) Honoring myself as the needy daughter, I grieve.

Interestingly, in all three gospels, the story of another daughter is encased within this one—the story of the woman with a hemorrhage. This daughter, sharing my story of painful abandonment, was no longer a child. Empowered by her own desire, she reached toward wholeness, toward Jesus, and found new life.

Heal me, O God, and I will be healed.
Save me, and I will be saved.
Fill me with the courage to grieve,
to embrace my own power, and to boldly love
the little ones around me. Amen.

L. RUTH WASHINGTON is a woman in her "middle" years seeking to live into the truth that she cannot love others until she has chosen to love herself—a critical lesson for someone who cares for others professionally as well as within her home. She loves to garden, explore Scripture, and host very fancy lunches for women friends.

Monday of Lent I
Psalm 63

> *O God, you are my God, I seek you, my soul thirsts for*
> *you; my flesh faints for you, as in a dry and weary land*
> *where there is no water. . . . your steadfast love is better*
> *than life . . . my mouth praises you with joyful lips . . . for*
> *you have been my help, and in the shadow of your wings*
> *I sing for joy. My soul clings to you; your right hand*
> *upholds me.*
>
> *Psalm 63:1, 3a, 5b, 7–8*

The rapture, the passion, of this psalm are akin to the most breathtaking romantic poetry. Could Shakespeare surpass its intensity? This may startle us. Romantic poetry belongs in the world of the flesh, does it not? We are brought up to believe that the kind of longing for complete union that it expresses, the surrender of self, is meant for our mortal loves and life partners. How much of the disappointment of romance and marriage goes back to this preconception?

Many of us seek fulfillment of self in union with other people throughout our lives—a quest that is met time and again with frustration and failure. On the other hand, we approach God with formality and structure—confusing distance with reverence.

Our psalmist poet sets us straight, tells the truth: only God merits and can sustain these feelings from us. Only with God can we find the flawless love and unfailing support that our souls crave. God's support has infinite facets and nuances. God cradles us, accepts us as we are, abides with us, consoles us, nurtures us, encourages us, stands behind us, affirms us, sustains us. God is our constant companion, the alpha and omega of our lives as well as of the cosmos, the One Infinite, the One Sublime.

God of Love, grant me the wisdom and the courage
to seek you with unbounded passion.
Help me open myself to the full mystery of your Love
and to offer to you joyfully that which is already yours—
my destiny. Let my life be a song of praise to your glory. Amen.

+ SUSAN J. BARNES has a Ph.D. in art history. After a career in museum
work, she received a call to ministry and was ordained in the Diocese
of Texas in June 2001. She serves a parish in Austin, Texas.

Tuesday of Lent I
Mark 4:1–21

When someone lights a lamp, does he put a box over it to
shut out the light? Of course not! The light couldn't be seen
or used. A lamp is placed on a stand to shine and be useful.
Mark 4:21–22

I read a story once about an obstetrician and a couple about to have their first child. The obstetrician learned that the expectant father was a musician and told him how he envied him, because he had always wanted to be a musician. As the pregnancy progressed, complications developed and the husband rushed his wife to the hospital, where the obstetrician performed an emergency caesarian section. When the surgery was over, the obstetrician was explaining the complications to the new father and told him the seriousness of the condition. The physician assisting him in the operating room interrupted their conversation to tell the obstetrician that he had performed brilliantly in the operating room, and that it was an honor for him to have assisted him.

The new father, recalling their conversation, was confused and said, "You told me that you always wanted to be a musician. How can you say that when you just saved the lives of my wife and my baby and you have the admiration and respect of your colleagues?"

The obstetrician told him, "Yeah, I was pretty good in there all right, and I know why. Today I awakened two hours early and played Chopin on my piano."

The moral to this story is that when we allow ourselves the time during our busy day to do the things we really love doing, the joy and enthusiasm we derive from it permeate all other aspects of our lives. We can perform brilliantly in the tasks that we *have* to do because we have allowed ourselves the gift of doing the things that give special meaning and value to our lives.

I have heard it said, and I think it is particularly true for women, that most people are less afraid of being a failure than being a success. Our dreams and aspirations seem to be inhibited by our fear of being successful. And yet, Jesus is telling us to "shine" and be "useful." Whatever talents we have should be unashamedly practiced and displayed. In doing so, we will be using the talents God gave us to enhance our lives and be an example of his glorious handiwork.

The Lenten season is traditionally a time of mortification. More recently we have been encouraged to put positive practices into our Lenten observance. I will use it as a time of gratification, doing those things that God has given me the talent to do well, those things that I really enjoy doing. Perhaps in doing so, I can restore joy and enthusiasm to the other aspects of my life. I can shine and be useful.

MARY CATHERINE COUSINS is a divorced, working woman with two lovely grown daughters whose life can be described as a frustrating struggle. But life thus far has taught her that service to others is a privilege and adversity can be a blessing, that a life well reflected upon can be viewed as humorous, and that in order to see joy and goodness in others you must first recognize it in yourself. Her personal life motto is: "Have fun!"

Wednesday of Lent I
Luke 2:36–38

> *There was also a prophet, Anna, the daughter of Phanuel,*
> *of the tribe of Asher. She was of a great age, having lived*
> *with her husband seven years after her marriage, then as*
> *a widow to the age of eighty-four. She never left the tem-*
> *ple but worshiped there with fasting and prayer night and*
> *day. At that moment she came, and began to praise God*
> *and to speak about the child to all who were looking for*
> *the redemption of Jerusalem.*
>
> *Luke 2:36–38*

Secluded, restricted, marginalized, confined to "Women Only" areas, limited literally and theologically by religious authorities, yet described in Scripture as a "prophet." How extraordinary! A visible role model for women: standing fast in the midst of doubters; risking judgment from a patriarchal community; being willing to be an object of derision; worshiping in her own meaningful way; encountering the divine personally; expressing her gratefulness; telling her story!

Blessings upon you my sister, Anna. From deep within your soul, God brought forth your gifts of perseverance, of tenacity, of courage to stand alone. Day after day your prayers permeated the area like incense. Did you hear the voices? "Crazy old woman . . . stubborn . . . senile perhaps . . . why can't she be like the rest of us?" Yet you persisted, focused, single-minded.

Blessings upon you my sister, Anna. From deep within your soul God brought forth your gift of patience. Scanning the crowds daily. Waiting with such assurance that God's love would be revealed.

Blessings upon you my sister, Anna. From deep within, God brought forth your gift of proclamation. At long last the conviction became a reality. How you must have laughed with delight at the baby, the Christ child. To cradle God in your arms! Your heart warmed with gratitude. As you looked deep into his eyes, your soul filled with divine love, love that, once experienced, must be shared.

Creator God, thank you for the legacy of our foremothers.
When we despair, help us to connect with their strengths.
Reach deep into our souls and bring forth our innate gifts.
Give us courage to share our stories, our revelations of God's love.
Let us leave a legacy of love to our descendants. Amen.

LILLIAN SMITH THARP is a late bloomer, forced out of dormancy into flower by Disciple Bible Study, United Methodist Women, Stephen Ministry, and life circumstances. She is grateful to Brigid's Place for providing the ideal climate for continuous growth.

Thursday of Lent I
Psalm 42

Kathleen Norris, in her memoir *The Cloister Walk*, quotes Evagrius: "Anger is given to us by God to help us confront true evil." What a radical revision for me to consider! I am uncomfortable with anger, my own and that directed toward me. Like so many women, I was raised to believe that keeping the peace was a religious obligation: If someone got angry with me, I was to blame—and if I became angry, I had sinned.

Evagrius reminds me that anger can be a gift, a means of articulating and responding to injustice, and the psalmist rails against "those who are deceitful and unjust." But what about anger directed toward God? The Psalter here is full of comfort. In Psalm 42, God is challenged and is called to justification: "Why have you forgotten me?" Jesus repeated these words at the time of his execution. They are angry, accusatory, desperate, and finally beseeching.

Sometimes my frustrations with myself, with others, and with the terrible griefs and injustices of this world lead me to cry out against God. I am tired of accepting God's will and impatient with a mind that cannot grasp God's mysteries. I am learning to follow the psalmist and Jesus and to bring all of those emotions to God—my anger, my confusion, my desperation. There is no piety in trying to hide them; there is only a peaceful emptying when my disquieted soul can join with God. With oneness of heart I can again call God my hope and my help.

MARTHA SERPAS, a graduate of Yale Divinity School and the University of Houston's doctoral program in creative writing, teaches writing, religion, and literature at the University of Tampa. She is a poet.

Kathleen Norris. *The Cloister Walk* (New York: Riverhead Books, 1996).

Friday of Lent I
Psalm 98

Sing a New Song

O God of all creation,
    hear our cries.
We thirst for action.
We thirst for justice.
Creator God, quench our thirst.

Chaos swirls about.
Doubt clouds our vision.
Rhetoric dulls our hearing.
Our hearts are bruised by modern-day Pharisees.
Will circumstances change?
How long must we wait?
When, when, O Lord?
When will there be new ways of thinking, new wine?
When will compassion infuse the darkness of distrust and prejudice?
When will all God's children be honored as they are created?
When will statements such as "Love the sinner, hate the sin"
    be recognized as obscenities?
When will women, men, and children *all* (not some) be granted
    freedom to be their true selves created in the image of God?
When will the new grapes of compassion be ripe?
O God, Keeper of the Vineyard,
    only you can provide the new grapes.
Let them be kissed with the sunlight of your love.
Let the Holy Spirit blow gently through the vineyard.
Select grapes of courage, inclusiveness, compassion.
May the blend provide sweetness of charity and clarity.
May the bouquet cause others to yearn for this new wine.

O God, Seamstress of New Wineskins,
    fashion the church universal for your purposes.
Make of it a container worthy of this new wine.
Lace it with stitches of Strength, of Righteousness,
    of Grace, and of Hope.

O God, our Wine Steward,
    let it be soon.
Use this Lenten season to prepare us.
Creator God, quench our thirst!

LILLIAN SMITH THARP is a late bloomer, forced out of dormancy into flower by Disciple Bible Study, United Methodist Women, Stephen Ministry, and life circumstances. She is grateful to Brigid's Place for providing the ideal climate for continuous growth.

Saturday of Lent I
Psalm 80

> *O LORD God of hosts, how long will you be angered despite*
> *the prayers of your people? You have fed them with the*
> *bread of tears; you have given them bowls of tears to drink.*
> *You have made us the derision of our neighbors, and our*
> *enemies laugh us to scorn. Restore us, O God of hosts; show*
> *the light of your countenance, and we shall be saved.*
>
> *Psalm 80:4–7*

In her commentary on the Book of Psalms, Kathleen Farmer likens the flow of life depicted in the psalms to an ocean wave. She says: "Assurance and doubt can wash back and forth over the faithful . . . The transition from anxiety to assurance in the psalms, as in human life, is not always neatly or permanently made." As far as life is concerned, this is indeed an understatement.

Recently I returned from a tranquil interlude in the mountains of Colorado. I spent a whole week gazing out the windows of my rented condo at a sparkling glacial lake surrounded by the Rocky Mountains. It was easy in this setting to feel sure that all was right with the world. Like the writer of Psalm 80, I could imagine the Sacred One as a shepherd, leading us like her flocks and shining forth upon the world.

Upon my return, however, I found that in just the short week I had been gone, a friend's only child had been killed in a car accident, another friend had been diagnosed with a rare and potentially lethal malady at the age of twenty-seven, and yet another friend's young nephew had gone to bed a happy and healthy child and died in his sleep. Gone was my sense of assurance in the rightness of things. Cast into anxiety by all this dreadful news, I could identify with the psalmist's question to God, "How long will you be angry?" Surely the beautiful and poignant images of being fed the bread of tears and given bowls of tears to drink are not too strong for what we feel at times like these.

In the second half of Psalm 80, the speaker remembers a happier time of God's graciousness when she felt planted and tended like a precious vine. Now she asks God: "Why have you broken down its wall, so that all who pass by pluck off its grapes?" Times were good and now they are bad and whose fault is it? My twenty-first-century worldview does not allow me the luxury of blaming it all on an angry, omnipotent supreme being. It is just not that simple. Because at the same time all this sadness is taking place in the world, the mountains and that mystical glacial lake are still there. All of it exists in the loving embrace of the mystery that we call God.

PATTY SPEIER is the executive director of the Seton Cove Interfaith Spirituality Center. She is a spiritual director who specializes in the use of literature and writing to teach ethics and spiritual development, and is adjunct professor of pastoral ministries at the Episcopal Theological Seminary of the Southwest.

Kathleen A. Farmer, "Psalms," in *The Women's Bible Commentary*, ed. Carol A. Newsom and Sharon H. Ringe (Louisville, Ky.: Westminster/John Knox Press, 1992), 141.

Second Week of Lent

SECOND WEEK OF LENT

Second Sunday of Lent
Matthew 15:21–28
Mark 7:24–30

I t was an unlikely encounter. The Canaanite woman had no business approaching Jesus—no business speaking to him. They were
worlds apart: Jesus, a Jewish rabbi in a foreign land, and she, a
Canaanite from the district of Tyre and Sidon. She was seen as a hardened pagan, an enemy of the Jewish people. And she was a woman; the
behavioral codes in Near Eastern culture frowned on women and men
socializing.

Yet, in her boldness, we cannot but be drawn to her. When she
opens her mouth, her words have a ring of truth to them. She says,
"Have mercy on me, Lord, Son of David." She calls Jesus "Lord." She
knows of the Jewish messiah who preaches good news to the poor, who
heals the sick. She has heard of Jesus' great power and miracles among
his own people. And she believes that he is capable of healing her
demon-possessed daughter, if he but would.

Here is a mother after my own heart. She is willing to step out in a
way that was socially, politically, and religiously incorrect. She is willing to take abuse and ridicule in order to be heard. She wants the
demons exorcised from her daughter, and standing before her is the
man who can do it.

But Jesus explains that he was sent only to the people of Israel. It
would not be right to take that which was meant for the Jewish nation
and give it to her, a pagan. Then he hears her say: "Yes, Lord, yet even
the dogs eat the crumbs that fall from their masters' table." She
acknowledges her position as secondary to the children of Israel. Yet
her understanding of God's mercy and compassion is so encompass-
ing that even though the chosen children receive the food first, she sees

a way for her daughter to receive a portion of God's abundance. Jesus heals her daughter instantly.

It was an unlikely encounter—but one that God used to transform a woman, her possessed child, and even God's own Son.

+ NANCY DEFOREST is a priest on the staff of St. John the Divine Episcopal Church in Houston, Texas. Before being called to ordained ministry, she worked as an educator for twenty-two years.

Monday of Lent II
Jeremiah 22:13–23

Jeremiah speaks of the poor and needy, of building one's "house" on the foundation of injustice, of practicing oppression and violence. Who are the poor, the oppressed, the violated in our community today? Look around you. There is great spiritual poverty in our society and in our churches. Too many of us fail to view the other, especially the *different* other, as God's own beloved child, created by God and in God's image, bearing God's holy essence, worthy of our time, attention, and love. Look around you. Someone is always being violated—physically, emotionally, spiritually, economically—by hatred, prejudice, brute force, abuse of power, denial of human rights and dignity. As members together in the family of God, do we experience our intimate connection with them through compassion, or do we shut our eyes and ears to their pain? Look around you. Some persons are continually oppressed, hindered from experiencing more than a taste of the fulfillment God wills for them—and they certainly are not allowed to experience it fully. And why is this? Because others, fearing loss of their own power and privilege, oppress in order to keep these marginalized ones in bondage to things like skin color, accent, socioeconomic status, nationality, sexual orientation, political or denominational affiliation, education, gender.

Yet I do not lose heart, because Scripture asserts that God is on the side of these "least" ones. When I truly open myself, God *does* revive my heart and restore my hope. This sense of well-being emerges in different ways to meet needs in different situations. At times it is mediated through friends or strangers, nature, words of affirmation in Scripture, or writings of persons who refuse to be bound by the systemic injustice in which we daily live.

The biblical standard for judging the nations is their treatment of the "least"—the poor, widows, children, strangers, the powerless. I delight in glimpses of God's shalom that are tasted now and again, but hope and strive for a full experience of the kingdom of God.

+ GLYNDEN BODE is a Christian educator and an ordained deacon in the United Methodist Church in Houston, Texas.

Tuesday of Lent II
Psalm 80

> *Restore us, O LORD God of hosts; let your face shine, that*
> *we may be saved.*
>
> *Psalm 80:19*

There are difficult mountain times and steep valley times in life, rugged terrain emotionally, physically, and spiritually. The times of disconnects, invasions, and brokenness often seem the hardest in this wilderness called life. I hear the psalmist calling to God for restoration, for life.

My maternal grandmother, Ethel Rose, gave me a gift I now share with you. Granny lived into her mid-nineties, a petite, intense woman with a strong faith in God. I visited her in her Kansas City retirement center apartment, by myself, two years before she died. One afternoon she showed me what she had prepared and kept in her third dresser drawer—a blue shirtwaist dress for her burial (she always wore blue) and instructions to the young, new minister. Her written instructions for her funeral included the lines of the Twenty-third Psalm. Granny read the psalm to me. After the verse "Yea, though I walk through the valley of the shadow of death, I will fear no evil: for thou art with me; thy rod and thy staff they comfort me," she announced, "If there is a shadow, there must be a light!" Then she twinkled her blue eyes at me and said, "I thought of that myself." Granny's insight has stayed with me and will all the days of my life.

> Restore us, O LORD God of hosts;
> let your face shine, that we may be saved.

I seek to remember that if there is a shadow, there must be light. God's face shines. Our brother, Jesus Christ, is light sent into the world. When I focus on the light that shines on the objects blocking my way and on my resistances and fears, I have a different experience than when I focus on the objects, blockages, and fears. There is comfort and mystery in knowing that God's light in Christ shines on and embraces the difficult objects in life, and that the shadows are messengers of the presence of the light.

Restore us, O LORD God of hosts;
let your face shine, that we may be saved.

O Holy One of Light, Giver of Life, Blesser of the Way,
hold me in ways that I may know your ever-present love and light
as I prepare to receive anew the gift of life eternal in your light. Amen.

MARGUERITE (MEG) D. SCOTT is a marriage and family therapist, spiritual director, elder in the Presbyterian Church (U.S.A.), granddaughter, and spiritual life retreat leader who seeks labyrinths and walks in Christ's love.

Wednesday of Lent II
Mark 14:66–72
Matthew 26:69–75
Luke 22:54–62
John 18:15–17

> *One of the servant-girls of the high priest came by. When
> she saw Peter warming himself, she stared at him and
> said, "You also were with Jesus, the man from Nazareth."
> But he denied it, saying, "I do not know or understand
> what you are talking about."*
>
> *Mark 14:66*

Like the account of Judas's betrayal, there is an element of narrative
necessity in the account of Peter's denial of Jesus to the servant of
Caiaphas, the high priest. It seems that the characters had to play these
roles for the tragedy to unfold. This story appears in strikingly similar
form in all four gospels, but—apart from the obvious instinct for self-
preservation—none of the texts explains how Peter, one of Jesus' most
favored followers, could falter so miserably as to deny Jesus in the most
absolute terms at the moment of his mortal peril. Yet that's not very
different from me: I always intend to act and speak with love and
integrity, but so often experience the devastating recognition that my
words or actions have hurt or failed someone, even one I love deeply.

Peter, we are told, wept bitterly after fulfilling Jesus' prophecy of his
denial. The feelings experienced by the servant girl were not of interest
to the scrivener, an unfortunate fact since her powers of observation
are clearly engaged here. But it is the maid's confrontation that presents
Peter with a straightforward and dramatic choice: declare his loyalty
even if it means following Jesus to prison and death (as Peter had prom-
ised), or falsely deny his association with Jesus (as Jesus had predicted).
Seldom are the circumstances of my failures presented with such clarity or immediacy.

I am not Peter: the papacy is definitely not in my future, and I am unlikely to be called upon to die a martyr's death. Nevertheless, I find here the hope of grace to transcend my denials, failures, and falsehoods, to follow Jesus' way of absolute love.

PAMELA STOCKTON is a retired business lawyer and current student, with particular interests in contemplative spirituality and feminist theology.

Thursday of Lent II
Psalm 44

> *Awake, O Lord! why are you sleeping? Arise! do not reject*
> *us for ever. Why have you hidden your face and forgotten*
> *our affliction and oppression? We sink down into the dust;*
> *our body cleaves to the ground. Rise up, and help us, and*
> *save us, for the sake of your steadfast love.*
>
> *Psalm 44:23–26*

I stood in the tiny bedroom of my cave-like apartment, lost in the depth of my aloneness. Like the Israelites, I felt abandoned by God. No barrier shielded me from the affliction and oppression of the world. My husband had left Houston, left Texas, left me. My twenty-year-old son was away at college, angry and silent. My sixteen-year-old son sat closeted in his bedroom, rock music blasting his rage through the walls. And now, his car, which I had so carefully bought with the last of my savings, needed a ring job.

Over the months, I had fallen prey to the old theory of the *deus absconditus*, the God withdrawn, hidden, silent. Now, I wondered if God even existed.

I sank to the floor, unable to carry the burden alone any longer, my knees and heart cleaving to the ground. I folded my hands and began "to pray without ceasing." I opened up to all the pain, just asking God to listen. In the midst of my outpouring, the telephone rang.

"Are you okay?" asked a concerned voice I recognized as my former husband's.

"No," I admitted, finally able to show my vulnerability. "I'm not okay."

"I'm sorry," he said. "Somehow it'll be all right."

In that split second I knew beyond all knowing that God had heard me. Throughout my life I'd been told over and over again how God works in mysterious ways. But never had I expected to hear God's words through that man's voice. Thankful, I arose from my knees and went out to face another day, knowing I was not, nor had I ever been, alone.

May I remember in times of darkness
that Someone sits in that darkness with me,
hearing me, bringing me love when I take time to feel it
and bringing me light when I have eyes to see it.

SANDI STROMBERG is a professional writer and writing teacher who is senior communications specialist at M. D. Anderson Cancer Center and editor of *Network*, a quarterly publication that tells the stories of the center's patients. She is the former executive director of Brigid's Place.

Friday of Lent II
John 12:27–36

"Now my soul is troubled. And what should I say—
'Father, save me from this hour'? No, it is for this reason
that I have come to this hour. Father, glorify your name."
John 12:27

Jesus has just explained to Philip and Andrew that a solitary grain must fall into the ground and die if it is to bear a rich harvest, but they do not grasp the implications. His expression of inner turmoil reaches across the centuries to intersect poignantly with our own humanity. Hours that we might wish to be saved from but must live through—we all have them. What about a woman's final hour of labor? She dreads the pain yet longs for the child this hour will bring.

I will never forget the hour in April 1978 when I was scheduled to have a breast biopsy, to be followed immediately by a radical mastectomy if the tumor was malignant.

The week before, my soul was in turmoil. How could this be happening to me? I was only thirty-seven! Wasn't it just older women who got breast cancer? Why hadn't my gynecologist gotten excited about this lump nine months earlier when I had first pointed it out to him? How would my husband react? What about my children? My students? And overarching all, did I or didn't I have breast cancer? And if I did, how would I endure such disfigurement? I groped through the days, gathering information, choosing a surgeon, confiding in close friends and requesting prayers, trying to remain optimistic yet realistic, arranging childcare, contacting colleagues to cover my classes. I dreaded the hour to come, but it was this hour I had come to.

When I regained consciousness, my body was racked with waves of pain and nausea. The left side of my chest felt as if a six-inch strip of sheet metal had been pounded into it. A priest hovered over me, praying. He pressed my right hand into a balled fist, and the sharp edges of some object dug into my palm. It was a cross—a raft to carry me across this river of loss and pain.

The following year held many more hours I might have rejected but lived through with God's help: hours of radiation therapy and chemotherapy, hours of vulnerability and uncertainty. Hours that gave birth to the rest of my life.

Thank you, Holy One.

MARTHA WEATHERS taught literature and composition for over twenty years for the Houston Community College System, where she also served several terms as department head. Now retired, she enjoys having time to write and do volunteer work.

Saturday of Lent II
Psalm 51:1–18

> *Create in me a clean heart, O God, and renew a right*
> *spirit within me.*
>
> *Psalm 51:10*

Christmas Eve was poisoned by the belligerence of one person. Kneeling purposefully in the center of the altar rail, he loudly refused the chalice I bore: "I don't recognize your ordination, and I will not receive communion from you." Even when one of my male colleagues offered him my chalice, he refused it: "I cannot even receive from the cup she has carried."

Poison. The man was entitled to his opinion, but he was not entitled to make a scene on Christmas Eve at the altar. I was angry at his rudeness, and I was angry with myself for giving his words the power to anger me.

The problem was that I felt it was impossible to confront his offense. I couldn't call him a jackass, and I couldn't kick him out of church. As I stewed, it occurred to me that I actually could have responded in those ways or worse. I had simply chosen a more appropriate response.

> Create in me a clean heart, O God,
> and renew a right spirit within me.

The prayer that I turned to that night was a prayer for God to clear away all the angry feelings within me that had been evoked by one man's venomous attack. There was probably nothing that I could do to change his heart, but it *was* in my power to work on mine.

Likewise, the season of Lent gives all of us an opportunity to purge ourselves of poison. There is no need to beat ourselves up—because we have all been created in God's image, even ordained women and belligerent men. Our job is simply to clean out the clutter in our lives so that we can be certain there is room for God.

+ ELIZABETH HOLDEN has served at Christ Church Cathedral in Houston since 1995 as Canon for Family Ministries. In addition to liturgical responsibilities, she works primarily with children and their families—a natural fit for this mother of two young children.

Third Week
of Lent

THIRD WEEK OF LENT

Third Sunday of Lent
Ruth 1:16–17

> *Wherever you go, I shall go, wherever you live, I shall live.*
> *Your people will be my people, and your God will be my*
> *God. Where you die, I shall die and there I shall be buried.*
> *Ruth 1:16–17*

These words vowing unending devotion are frequently heard at a marriage ceremony, but they are a pledge from a daughter-in-law to her mother-in-law. This kind of loyalty, faithfulness, and loving-kindness is called *chesed* in the Hebrew Bible. It comes not from any external legal obligation or social custom, but from inner faithfulness and grace.

Thinking about this deepest of friendships, I realize it is a gift that women give each other. Susan and I have shared that kind of friendship since we were in the fifth grade, forty-five years ago. We are different personalities, live thousand of miles apart, see each other perhaps once a year; but we meet on a "soul" level, even when we only talk on the phone. We are able to just "be" for each other, not judging, not trying to fix anything—even when her husband died suddenly at age forty-eight, or when my father died on the same day as her mother.

I don't think it takes a forty-five-year relationship or such traumatic events to find this kind of friendship. Women can be open enough to experience it with someone just met at a retreat. No matter how long the friendship, it is life-giving. Women are able to comfort, nurture, and listen each other into life. It is the relationship that the Creator has in mind for all of us and that Jesus so perfectly demonstrated. It seems to me that women have an innate ability for such a relating and that it is the path to healing and wholeness.

Creator God, I thank you for your gift of *chesed*,
and pray that we can recognize it as your being in us,
and share it with the world. I pray, too, that men may find
this gift in themselves, and share it as women do.
I believe it would heal the earth. Amen.

JUDY MOOD, president of Brigid's Place, is a "seeker" who has lived in the Far East, the Middle East, Europe, and Alaska. She currently resides in Houston, Texas, with her husband Rob.

Monday of Lent III
John 3:16–21

For God so loved the world, that he gave his only begotten Son, that whosoever believeth in him should not perish, but have everlasting life.

John 3:16

On May 7, 2000, I called my dear college friend, Becky. No answer. A few hours later, I received a phone call from her daughter that has been replayed many times since. Becky had died as she slept in her own bed, overlooking her beautiful backyard where she would have been most other Sunday afternoons. She had worked a full day for the State of Arkansas the previous Friday.

On Mother's Day weekend, 1998, Becky and her fifteen-year-old daughter, Avery, had come to visit from Little Rock. She shared with me that she "had lost the war, but had some more battles to fight" in her decade-long struggle with cancer. I wept most of the weekend. She wept some. However, most of the time she lived in a bigger space, one that knew that "everlasting life" of which John speaks. She kept saying, "It'll all work out," cocking her head with a knowing smile. She had come with a purpose, to ask me if I would be Avery's guardian. After Avery and I returned home from walking around the Transco fountain, Becky's watery eyes met mine as she said, "See?"

My vision was not as clear as hers. I was not as far along my faith walk as Becky. When the call came, her words came through: "The victory's won. Turn all your attention onto Avery." That entire week, I felt that Becky was never far from us. Her college roommate and my friend, Jody, came from Washington. We laughed, we cried, we felt her presence, we were embraced by God. Together, the many arrangements and decisions fell into place as we walked through that prayerful, grieving space between heaven and earth.

Through the years, Becky has given me many gifts, material and nonmaterial. Nothing compares to her reawakening John's gospel for me, symbolized by a light that streamed through a previously unknown skylight and bathed my husband and me as we sang during her funeral, "We will raise her up." It serves as a continual reminder of living life in faith, rather than investing in a particular outcome. Becky believed. She passed the peace to her friend.

JENNIFER EMBRY spent sixteen years in the business community as a landman with an independent oil company and as a vice president of a savings and loan. She has recently received her master's degree in counseling psychology at Pacifica Graduate Institute.

Tuesday of Lent III
Psalm 50

If you call upon Me in times of trouble, I am ever present
to you. You will know Me in your hearts.

Psalm 50:15
Psalms for Praying *by Nan C. Merrill*

As we sat in the hospital room that morning, my husband was gently brushing my hair down my back. We were quiet—not talking, for once. It had been a long and difficult journey to this moment. My twin brother needed a kidney and, being the only sibling, I felt my name had been called. My husband was not thrilled with the idea, concerned about the possible effects of this major surgery. There had been some tearful times over the decision, but I knew from the moment I was declared a match that I would be donating a kidney.

Many excruciating tests had to be passed. They don't just "let" you give a kidney. There were some setbacks, and my husband began to come around. By the time I had to undergo the arteriogram, he was rooting for me. So now it was the morning of the surgery, and they would be coming for me soon to "harvest" the kidney. I began to feel an incredible peace, such as I had never experienced before. I felt surrounded by a circle of warmth and light. I knew my family and all my friends at home in Alaska were praying for us, and I could actually feel it. I knew, at that moment, that everything would be all right.

Looking back, I know that the connection of the Spirit of Love in me with the Spirit of Love in them created that sublime moment of peace. I believe that is what prayer is, and how it works.

Beloved Creator, you are always with us, and sometimes,
when we are quiet, we can truly know it in our hearts.

JUDY MOOD, president of Brigid's Place, is a "seeker" who has lived in the Far East, the Middle East, Europe, and Alaska. She currently resides in Houston, Texas, with her husband Rob.

Nan C. Merrill, *Psalms for Praying: An Invitation to Wholeness* (New York: Continuum, 2001).

Wednesday of Lent III
Tobit 7

> *She wept for her daughter. Then, wiping away the tears,*
> *she said to her, "Take courage, my daughter; the Lord of*
> *heaven grant you joy in place of your sorrow. Take*
> *courage, my daughter." Then she went out.*
>
> *Tobit 7:16*

Edna and Raguel's daughter, Sarah, has had seven husbands. Each husband has died on his wedding night. On this night, Edna prepares Sarah's room to receive her eighth husband, Tobias.

Edna has witnessed her daughter suffer unimaginable grief. She cries for Sarah, yet there is nothing she can do to protect her from either past or future sorrow. Edna weeps, but makes no false or sentimental promise, though the temptation may have been there in the tears. Instead, she invites Sarah to find courage.

How many times have I wished my mother could have protected me from life's sorrows? Invisible arms slaying my dragons and keeping me safe and warm—such were my hopeful expectations. Instead, my sorrows came. My mother provided me with encouragement and her unwavering faith. All of this time, though, I haven't known how to hear my mother's voice.

In the back of my mind I hear Edna's quiet reminder that it takes courage to allow joy to replace sorrow. I hear Edna's voice, and now I hear something new. I hear my mother's quiet encouragement to allow joy to replace my sorrow. It feels as though, once again, she is giving me the gift of life.

AMY ROWLAND is a writer and philosopher who currently lives in Houston, Texas.

Thursday of Lent III
Psalm 24

> Who can ascend the hill of the LORD and who can stand
> in his holy place? Those who have clean hands and a pure
> heart, who have not pledged themselves to falsehood, nor
> sworn by what is a fraud.
>
> *Psalm 24:3–4*

Like many rhetorical questions in the Bible, this one seems at first glance to be just another guilt-inducing aphorism. After all, which of us can live up to the answer? Life is a messy business; few of us can claim the innocence that the words "clean hands" and "pure heart" seem to imply. But if we can sit with the tension of this question long enough to get past the initial reaction of guilt, the deep-seated fear that we are not good enough to ascend that hill, then we can begin to open to the good news of this passage.

The good news is that we are right now, this very minute, in God's holy place. We are, in this present moment and in every moment, as Hildegard of Bingen states, "wrapped in the arms of the mystery of God." Then why do we often feel that we are stuck in the foothills with little hope of ascension? The psalm supplies a clear answer. We have bought into the falsehood that we are somehow unworthy of the Gracious One's presence; we have sworn allegiance to a system of false selves designed to keep us in our place (at the bottom of the hill). We gain the summit not by some arduous self-improvement regimen, but by simply waking up to the realization that we are precious in the sight of the Heart of Love. We move the cause of redemption further when we say "Yes" to Love's invitation, claim our rightful place on the top of the hill, and open our eyes to the vista spread before us.

> Gracious Love, I open the gates of my heart to the knowledge
> that I am precious, intensely loved, and desired by you.

PATTY SPEIER is the executive director of the Seton Cove Interfaith Spirituality Center. She is a spiritual director who specializes in the use of literature and writing to teach ethics and spiritual development, and is adjunct professor of pastoral ministries at the Episcopal Theological Seminary of the Southwest.

Friday of Lent III
Luke 19:41–48

> *When he came in sight of [Jerusalem], he wept over it and*
> *said, "If only you had known . . . the way that leads to*
> *peace! . . . For a time will come upon you, when your ene-*
> *mies will set up siege-works against you . . . and not leave*
> *you one stone standing on another, because you did not*
> *recognize God's moment when it came."*
> *Luke 19:41–44*

Jesus weeps when we do not recognize God's moment when it comes. The Christ within cries out in anguish when life leaves us without a stone standing and we find ourselves without the peace to sustain.

When I divorced in early 1992, I, like most women, faced new crossroads. From all appearances, I was in a good place—no responsibilities for children, exciting career, comfortable home, wonderful friends, active and interesting life, free of cancer for nearly five years. My marriage years had been, in many ways, good for my outer life. I had honed my business and social skills, traveled a lot, advanced my career. But despite the exterior bounty, I had starved my soul nearly to death, and I was suffering deeply for it. I couldn't recognize God's moments, and I knew it.

I don't believe in spiritual formulae anymore. I believe God presents each of us with opportunities for redemption, and, like Jerusalem, we either name them or not, embrace them or not. We can't anticipate those moments—we can only become ready as best we can and pray for the grace that we will experience God. We ready our lamps with the enlightening oil of inner work. We feed the soul in the inner world—in meditation, prayer, study, reading, psychoanalysis or therapy, creative arts, woolgathering, dream work, thinking, dialoguing. Each one's way is unique and belongs to her alone. We commit to know, to love, to become ourselves, and to stay with it. All moments are God's moments, and through grace we come to recognize some of them. Our lives gradually begin to reflect more accurately who we really are, and we find our own meaning. We truly do experience God. These promises are not empty. They are full to overflowing.

The process is frightening, difficult, dangerous, painful, and consuming of both time and energy. It is also comforting, transforming, clarifying, deeply satisfying, and is the source of inner peace.

> The earth is the LORD'S and all that is in it,
> the world, and those who live in it. (*Psalm 24:1*)

LOIS ANN PECKHAM lived a rich, textured, happy, reconciled life full of love and she died well (her words) in July 1999. Many remember her today with much affection—she was courageous, intelligent, and, especially, a good friend.

Saturday of Lent III
Psalm 72

> *May you heed the cry of the poor—the young and the*
> *old, setting free all those in need. . . . May fears that*
> *imprison the people be brought to the Light, and rise*
> *from the depths!*
>
> *Psalm 72:4a, 9*
> Psalms for Praying *by Nan C. Merrill*

Our cousin George had been paralyzed by pain in his back from a car accident for five years when he heard that an operation might free his compressed spinal nerves and relieve that unrelenting pain. This might enable him to do the therapy that could help him walk again. However, George had struggled through several sieges of pneumonia in past years, and there was considerable risk in having surgery at all—and no guarantee that it would work. What a decision to make. Many of us had been praying for him, with laying on of hands for healing, and many had been praying and sending him the energy of their love from afar. When Jesus told the paralyzed man to stand, take up his mat, and walk, that man had to make a decision to be bold and trust this strange one who challenged him. George, too, had to be bold and brave to risk possible death for the possibility of a new pain-free life with the hope of walking again. We rejoice with him and his family that his faith overcame fear—he had the surgery and became pain free. What a tremendous relief.

In Psalm 72 we hear the psalmist beseeching God to heed the cry of the young and old, setting free all in need so that the fears that imprison them may "be brought to the Light, and rise from the depths." What are the fears that paralyze you and me? Are we afraid for our children and grandchildren? Do we worry about the threat of domestic violence in their homes and violence in their schools and their communities? Perhaps we see ways to help, but fear we would be intruding, or making them angry with us, or even making things worse.

When I open my heart to Jesus, spend time
in silence with him, and ask him to set me free from my fears,
my trust that God is working still in my life and in theirs grows.
I can believe that they cannot fall out of the net of God's love.
Then I can believe that prayer is my most important work,
and that if more is needed I will be guided
to bold and useful action. Amen.

+ DIANE BRELSFORD is an Episcopal parish priest in the Diocese of
Olympia, Washington. She is currently the co-convener of Episcopal
Peace Fellowship in the diocese. She was formerly a hospice chaplain
and mentor for Education for Ministry.

Nan C. Merrill, *Psalms for Praying: An Invitation to Wholeness* (New York: Continuum, 2001).

Fourth week
of Lent

FOURTH WEEK OF LENT

Fourth Sunday of Lent
Judges 4:1–22, 5:1–31

D eborah—judge, prophet, military leader—was a woman of considerable influence and privilege. As I read the account of Deborah's role in Israel's victory over the Canaanites, I struggle to decipher what Deborah has to offer me as a woman of faith. Certainly I admire a woman of such strength, who so ably delivers her people from twenty years of oppression. But I am repulsed by Deborah's methods and by the implication that this bloody conquest was God's bidding.

The concept of divine retribution has never been a part of my spiritual thought processes. Maybe this story is meant to be a reminder of the ways in which I misuse my influence or fail to use my gifts in peaceful and constructive ways. Perhaps it is a call to examine all of my options before acting out of anger or frustration.

Last summer we moved to the country. We bought a wonderful house on two acres—lots of running room for the children. Before moving, we had carefully checked out the local elementary school that would be attended by two of our children, and had high hopes that the school would live up to its reputation. But this school has been a nightmare for our nine-year-old adopted daughter, who is African-American and who, for the first time in her life, has met with rampant racism. We're removing our daughter from the school and plan to homeschool her for the rest of the year. That's the easy part. The hard part is restraining my impulse to storm the houses of the children who have done this to our daughter and demand retribution. But I am reminded by Deborah that I am called instead to be a reconciling and life-giving force—even in the midst of oppression.

Gentle Wisdom, we live in a world so tainted
by violence and the misuse of power.
As women of faith, we are molded in your strong image.
Help us use that strength in ways
that bring peace and understanding. Amen.

SUZANNE BYERLY and her partner are co-parents of six children ranging
in age from two to twenty-seven. Suzanne is an attorney who currently
works as a lay minister for her Lutheran congregation.

Monday of Lent IV
Psalm 56

You have kept count of my tossings; put my tears in your
bottle. Are they not in your record?

Psalm 56:8

I remember the day when I realized that I had forgotten how to cry. I tried to remember the last time tears had come to my eyes. What had happened to the spontaneous little girl who expressed her emotions so freely—one who laughed and cried and sang and danced and hugged and gave big, sloppy kisses?

As an aspiring, young professional woman straight out of grad school, I had the impression that showing emotion was a sign of female weakness. To survive in a male-dominated profession, I surmised that I would have to learn how to think and act like a man. After ten years of containing my emotions, I found myself at the point of complete burnout. Slowly, I began the long, healing journey to excavate the latent emotional essence of my female self that had long since been abandoned.

Jesus was comfortable with his own tears and openly wept when he felt the sorrow of his friends grieving the loss of Lazarus. He also lamented the loss of faith of his own people. The psalmist reminds us that God is intimately aware of our inner tossings and turmoils. And certainly God welcomes our honest tears.

Thank you, Creator and Sustainer of life,
for giving us the emotional release valve and cleansing of tears.
In you we experience wholeness and fullness.
Today, help us to see our emotions as proof that we
are fully alive and connected to you, others, and the world. Amen.

+ PAMELA L. TAYLOR is currently a hospital chaplain. Over the past twenty-five years of ministry, she has also served as a youth minister, college campus minister, and hospice chaplain.

Tuesday of Lent IV
Exodus 4:10–20, 27–31

> *Moses said, "O God, I have never been eloquent, neither*
> *in the past nor since you have spoken to your servant. I am*
> *slow of speech and tongue." God said to him, "Who gave*
> *you your mouth? . . . makes you deaf or mute? gives you*
> *sight or makes you blind? Is it not I, the Almighty? Now*
> *go; I will help you speak and will teach you what to say."*
> *Exodus 4:10–12*

This passage from Exodus really bothered me. I see so much of myself in Moses. I, too, consider myself to be ineloquent. I even have a sister who, like Aaron, is eloquent, eloquent enough to write poetry that others praise and that often I don't understand. I consider myself to be so inarticulate that here I am at the last minute—late actually—just now sitting down to write this meditation, having put it off until the shame of total failure and the certain disappointment of my editor prodded me to the computer. Of course, merely passable writing is not my only fault. I have many others, which came tumbling into my brain as I thought on this passage. And as I was musing on my many failings I felt shame: shame at my critique of my Creator. I am not good enough for myself even though God thinks me good enough for all of creation. That perhaps is my greatest fault—pride—the pride that makes me believe I know better than God what my strengths and weaknesses are. It is this same pride that keeps me from trying new things. How often do I choose not to explore my potential? How often do I stick to the story that it is my sister who is eloquent, my mother and other sister who are beautiful, my husband who is smart, or my father who was brave? How often am I the one who is none of those things, who is Nobody? I am ashamed to say that I often think all of those things. It is all a fabrication, my story, and it separates me from God. The story keeps me from being all that God created me to be.

This Lenten season I will try to change the story, to expand it to include those things that I thought I wasn't or couldn't do. I will try new things and I will fail and I will accomplish and I will be more fully human.

O Creator, you have made Cindy Crawford,
Stephen Hawking, Mother Teresa,
and me in your image, and for that I am thankful.
Push away the sin of pride that separates me from you.
Help me to remember that your most gracious gift is life itself,
with all of its struggles and successes.
Help me to rejoice in life, not fear or critique it.
Most of all, help me to see me as you see me,
as your most beloved and precious creation,
whom you shaped in the womb and knew would exist
from the beginning of time, and who is perfect in your sight.
In the name of your loved Son. Amen.

JENNIFER PADEN is a "cradle" Episcopalian, and now a church employee. She has a degree in psychology from the University of Houston.

Wednesday of Lent IV
Acts 12:11–17

Validate me, please!

Rhoda, a maid in the house of Mary, John Mark's mother, had been praying all night for Peter, who had been thrown into prison by Herod. She heard a knock on the door. She didn't open it (wise, when Herod was stalking his Christian prey), but asked, "Who's there?" She knew Peter well enough to recognize his voice, and her excitement at hearing it propelled her to run and tell the household. She left Peter outside knocking!

Because I am one who loves to be the first to tell, who wants the glory of anyone's big moment to rain down and saturate "me too!" I suspect Rhoda of that same hunger for validation. In my Rhoda-self, I am longing to have everyone light up with joy when I come with good news, to accept my role as a messenger from God with pure delight. I want to be acknowledged as a trustworthy and significant part of what's happening.

However, I see that my hunger for acknowledgment and a share of the limelight can cause me to do foolish things, things that could create some danger or certainly inconvenience for God's people whom I serve. If a soldier had come along and found Peter still on the doorstep, Rhoda's life could have been marked with tragedy.

I hope that she had a sense of humor more finely developed than my own—for surely that story was told over and over through the years, and Rhoda's leaving Peter on the doorstep was emphasized with shouts of laughter, shaking heads, and mutters of "scatterbrained woman." May Rhoda herself have continually remembered the incredulous joy that filled her soul when she knew their prayers were answered.

> Lord, like an innocent child I enter your kingdom exuberantly
> and expect to be greeted with delight!
> Forgive me when I want the same thing from
> my fellow man so much that I neglect to be wise. Amen.

NATHALIE SORRELL is a volunteer with Texas Reach Out Ministries, which brings healing to women leaving prison through the telling of their stories and through creative endeavors to help them re-envision their lives.

Thursday of Lent IV
Jeremiah 23:16–32

> *Do not listen to the words of the prophets who prophesy to you; they are deluding you. They speak visions of their own minds, not from the mouth of the LORD. They keep saying to those who despise the word of the LORD, "It shall be well with you"; and to all who stubbornly follow their own stubborn hearts, they say, "No calamity shall come upon you."*
>
> *Jeremiah 23:16–17*

Jeremiah boldly spoke out against false prophets—those who professed to speak for the Divine, but actually sought only to further their own agenda. As a Christian who is both a woman and a liberal, I find that the words of Jeremiah resonate with my late-twentieth-century experience.

There was a time—and quite a long time at that—that I refrained from calling myself "Christian," because the word conjured up images that were, to my understanding, wholly un-Christian. I was taught by "Christians" that I was to submit myself to another because of my gender, that capital punishment was God's will, that some were condemned to hell simply because of their affectional orientation, and that, overall, God was sickened by my sin. This simply did not square with my understanding of what it meant to be a follower of Jesus.

Rather, the Jesus I came to know was one who not only preached but also *practiced* a life of love, forgiveness, inclusivity, and self-sacrifice. In fact, according to the Scriptures, Jesus saved his judgmental comments exclusively for members of the religious establishment who prized their own authoritarian and patriarchal positions over the physical, social, and spiritual well-being of those around them. He chose instead to spend his time with social outcasts such as women, the sick, the poor, and those of socially unacceptable ethnic origins.

As we spend this season in contemplation of the meaning of the life of Jesus, let us also follow the example of Jeremiah, who worked boldly to bring the *true* message of the Divine to all people.

Divine Spirit, guide me to speak your words of justice and
peace in a world that is overgrown with prejudice and separatism.
Help me to offer love where there is hate;
inclusivity and acceptance where there is intolerance;
reconciliation where there is dissent. Amen.

BEVERLY RODGERS is a former attorney now pursuing a master of social
work degree. She has great admiration for women whose journey for
spiritual and intellectual fulfillment is a lifelong pursuit and hopes to
pass on that passion to her toddler daughter.

Friday of Lent IV
John 12:27–36

> "*Now my soul is troubled. And what should I say—*
> '*Father, save me from this hour*'*? No, it is for this reason*
> *that I have come to this hour.*"
>
> *John 12:27*

When I call out for help,
will I be heard?
And does the sound of my cry
mean anything to anyone but me?

Angry white-haired man sitting on his lofty throne—God of my youth,
can this Father hear my pleas?
Images of King, Lord, and Son of Man—
what do they know of lost fertility?

Are the girlhood fears of the dark
now the woman's fear of night?
My body knows the meaning of mortality—
who will hear and save me from this hour?

The sacrificial blood shed through the years, "It is finished."
In the passion of my becoming, I hear my cry.
Always it returns only to be heard by my ears.
Listening,
can I hear the voice of my self through the fear?

What would it be like if . . .

I dreamed about my mother last night. She decided on her own initiative to admit herself into treatment for her alcoholism. I realized that I didn't have to carry her cross for her any longer. She has heard her own cry for help. She has faced her darkness and chosen to move into the light. Interestingly enough, she looked a lot like me, only older.

JENNIFER ELKINS is a psychotherapist in private practice. Her interest in the interrelationship between women's spirituality and psychology shapes her perspective of the journey that each woman must choose in order to express her authenticity in the culture.

Saturday of Lent IV
Psalm 78:1–39

He divided the sea and led them through; he made the water stand firm like a wall. He guided them with the cloud by day and with light from the fire all night. He split the rocks in the desert and gave them water as abundant as the seas; he brought streams out of a rocky crag and made water flow down like rivers.

Psalm 78:13–16

There was a time when I counted the value of my days by what was happening in the lives of my loved ones. All bound up in a belief that others' time was more valuable, their accomplishments more significant, their pressures more severe, I lived a "secondary life." My own time, my unique gifts, and my precious resources didn't count as much as those of others.

One day, I was asked to draw my own lifeline and plot the moments in which God had intervened. Carefully, I marked the significant turning points along my lifeline. With a dawning reverence for my own life, I noted those times when God broke through and touched my life with grace and power.

Suddenly, it was as if I were taking my first breath. With my life spread out on a sheet of paper with all its ups and downs and ins and outs, I began to see that my assignment was not just to take a supporting role in the lives of others. My life task was to live my own life to the fullest. God was calling me to star in my own story, to breathe my own air, and to make my own music. And it was at that moment, deep within my soul, that the waters parted and I found within me what I needed to walk across the dry land from bondage to freedom.

Looking back, I also saw that God had been birthing me all along, watching over my comings and goings with tender, gentle, nurturing loving-kindness.

God-of-my-life . . . Creator, who birthed me . . .
help me to embrace all the various parts
of my own precious life as tenderly as you embrace me
and as quickly and willingly as I embrace others.
Give me the courage to receive the blessing you have for me,
and empower me to sing my own song freely
and fully all the days of my life. Amen.

JEANIE MILEY is a columnist, retreat leader, and speaker. She is the author of *The Spiritual Art of Creative Silence, Becoming Fire,* and *ChristHeart.*

Fifth Week
of Lent

FIFTH WEEK OF LENT

Fifth Sunday of Lent
Mark 5:25–34
Luke 8:43–48
Matthew 9:20–22

Twelve years she bled, though she did not die. Powerless as a woman: unclean and drained of energy. Nameless—some wags have dubbed her Flo. I prefer to call her Everywoman. Everywoman whose life has been poured out, drained, whose self-worth is determined by how much she does for others.

Everywoman because she lives in all of us. We give ourselves away so easily: Blood. Life. Energy. Time. Life blood. Meetings and committees, errands and busy-ness. Soon we discover we have been hemorrhaging. We have nothing left to give, and still the life drains out of us—a slow, steady drip. Giving without asking, giving without expecting anything in return, doing things out of duty, our lives drained away.

She did something brave, daring—and wonderful for all of us. Instead of doing the expected, the "nice" thing, she reached out and grasped what she wanted, what she needed. She did not even ask. She took. She bravely, boldly reached out to touch the hem of the One she believed to have the power to heal. She turned from what was slowly taking her life away and instead reached out for something that would *give* her life.

In reality, the healing may have begun when she heard of the Christ whose heart was soft even for the likes of her. Or perhaps some healing happened the moment she saw him and decided to reach out and touch that fringe.

We are told that Jesus felt the power leave him. Of course, she was empowered—as are we by her story. We, too, are invited to seek that which will stop the flow of our lives into nothingness and channel our energy into that which gives life to us and to others.

> God of great compassion, we thank you for this woman
> whose courage encourages us to evaluate our lives anew
> based on what gives us energy, joy, and life.
> Help us to let go of those things we do out of duty and "oughtness"
> so we may focus on that to which you alone call us,
> that for which we were uniquely and wonderfully made.
> In Christ's name, we pray. Amen.

+ SUSAN QUINN BRYAN is the pastor of A Community of the Servant-Savior, Presbyterian Church in America, and the mother of four daughters. She loves it when the women shine.

Monday of Lent V
John 4:43–54

In the miracle of the healed child, John recounts that an official begged Jesus to go with him to Galilee to cure his dying son. The disciple relates that this father believed Jesus when he said, "Go; your son will live." However, it was only after witnessing his child's recovered health that the man fully believed (perhaps in the broader strokes of divine love).

Often throughout my life I've considered this wobbly faith in holy guidance and healing. Why have I believed strongly only after obvious miracles? How very long it took me to realize that some sacred gifts initially appear as curses. My chronic illness seemed a curse until silent, reflective bed-times stretched lazily before me, allowing me the freedom and support to explore life's wealth. As soul-stretching exercised my inner life, I learned effective ways to cope, mature, and create meaningfully in my outer life.

A few years ago as Mardi Gras season unfolded (I lived my elementary-school days in New Orleans, so for me Lent is a natural culmination of weeks of festivities), I considered what I "should give up." Surprisingly, I realized I'd "given up" a great deal through the decades, even with a graceful flair at times. What I had difficulty doing was embracing the mystery of divine intervention. So, during that particular Lent and those that have followed, I sacrificed some pleasure and accepted a positive action related to it. One year I didn't buy books during Lent and revisited inspirational poems, stories, and essays already on my shelves. Another year I sacrificed cursing (which is my favorite ulcer-preventative) and embraced voicing gratitude as often as possible.

Letting go and sacrificing, along with accepting and embracing, seem like flip sides of the same coin. Reflecting on All That Is Sacred in my life, I simply flip the coin to discover a remarkable perspective . . . both sides are visible simultaneously when the curse is embraced as a healing miracle, and the miracle is accepted both as transitory and as automatically leading to new challenges.

Writer, teacher, watercolorist, and grandmother, SUZANNE SHELTON LIVINGSTON celebrates life on Gulf Coast beaches where the air is thick with "The Divine." She is completing her doctoral degree as a therapist focused on children with chronic and life-threatening illnesses.

Tuesday of Lent V
Psalm 40

> *I waited patiently upon the* LORD; *she stooped to me and*
> *heard my cry. . . . She put a new song in my mouth, a*
> *song of praise to our God. . . . Happy are they who trust*
> *in the* LORD!
>
> *Psalm 40:1–4*

I was driving to visit a man who is terminally ill, and it was raining so
hard I couldn't see very well and missed my turn off the freeway. The
area is rural with little lanes and indistinct names on the mailboxes.
Somehow, underneath this puzzlement and frustration, I had a sense
of peace and trusted I'd get there eventually.

When I did finally arrive at the driveway, I walked the prescribed
two hundred feet on a mysterious forest path, which provided a nice
meditative time for me to think about spiritual journeys to "where we
do not know." Then, in a clearing, I beheld a lovely, rustic, wooden
home with a Quonset-hut shape. I was welcomed by a warm, friendly
woman. As I entered this home, I saw the profile of a man sitting in
front of a large, antique window with small panes of glass. A majestic
black cat, also in profile, was sitting on the back of his chair. It struck
me that he looked like an archetypal Wisdom figure. I felt I had entered
one of those "thin places," where this tangible world and the spiritual
world interface with timeless values.

He and his wife were most cordial and welcoming. And so was the
cat. I noticed a buffalo head on the high wall behind him and also an
intriguing variety of feathered wall hangings and books on Native
American spirituality. We talked about the nurturing quality of this
connection to the Mother Earth Spirit and his creation-centered path
to God. I asked how he was doing and he said, "Really fine, although of
course I'm dying."

I felt honored for the gift of seeing his trusting, life-giving acceptance of the dying process. The three of us formed a circle and prayed
in thanksgiving for this family, their courage and trust in God's purpose and love. The deep peace of these people and that "thin place" has
stayed with me and nurtured me.

Mother Spirit, thank you for this experience.
Help us all to be alert for your surprises of joy. Amen.

+ DIANE BRELSFORD is an Episcopal parish priest in the Diocese of Olympia, Washington. She is currently the co-convenor of Episcopal Peace Fellowship in the diocese. She was formerly a hospice chaplain and mentor for Education for Ministry.

Wednesday of Lent V
Mark 6:17–29
Matthew 14:3–12

Put yourself into this unsettling account where you have the ability to treat another person as if he were expendable because he pointed out the truth to you. Herodias and her daughter, Salome, have the power to ask for the life of another, and Herod orders it to be done. It causes Jesus to withdraw to a deserted place by himself, probably to grieve and to ponder his own fate as he dares to speak the truth.

As in the story of the Pharisee and the publican, I thank God that I'm not like them . . . or am I? Where is my outrage when lives are taken or voices silenced because they speak the truth? Usually these voices have asked me to part with something, infringing on my comfort and security, so I am complicit while protecting my own position of privilege and power.

And what a sad example Herodias is for her daughter as she teaches her what it means to "please" others, not to mention demanding revenge. But Herod baffles me. In Mark's version, Herod *likes* to listen to John the Baptist and has the ultimate power to spare his life, but he is more concerned about not going back on his word in front of everyone and so acquiesces to the sickening request. I can relate to that as I recall times when I have covered up that which would expose my inadequacies.

I'm really not much different from these biblical characters except I'm not literally cutting off someone's head. But when I pass on that rumor, I take a bit of that person and put it on a platter. When I fail to speak up when I hear something offensive or an untruth about another, possibly another head ends up on a platter. Not a pleasant story, and one I would rather not think about because it calls me to look at my own Herod, Herodias, and Salome. It's much easier to point a finger at their evil than to claim it as my own.

Redeemer God, as I journey through Lent into Holy Week,
help me to trust that the miracle of Easter can redeem me from the
darkness in me which is difficult for the Light to expose. Amen.

PATTY TURNEY has her own business, is a spiritual director, and is a volunteer at Brigid's Place, where women are encouraged to find their voices and become empowered to meet the challenges of life.

Thursday of Lent V
Psalm 118
Jeremiah 23:16–32
Mark 8:31–9:1

All nations surround me . . . they surround me . . . they
surround me. . . . Out of my distress I called upon the
LORD. The LORD answered me and set me in a broad place.
Psalm 118:10, 5

They speak a vision of their own minds, not from the
mouth of the LORD.
Jeremiah 23:16b

"For you are setting your mind not on divine things but
on human things."
Mark 8:33b

Though I've never experienced an elevator-induced panic attack, I'm claustrophobic nonetheless. Recently, my supervisor called me into her office, inquiring about my work hours. It seems I misunderstood, thinking she had indicated some flexibility in the eight-to-five schedule. Although her tone was pleasant rather than challenging, I left the office with a sense of panic.

Narrow places. I love freedom and I hate narrow places. I love the feeling of wind in my hair. I become restless when I sense circumstances or people surrounding me. I hate feeling trapped—in rigid hours or demanding mortgages or a stagnant marriage.

I have learned that I am often more limited by my own passivity and fears than by the circumstances of life. I can choose to change jobs, move to a cheaper house, or relate to my husband differently. There is goodness in recognizing my freedom to exert control over many aspects of my life.

But is there more? At times, could there be *greater* good in choosing to remain in narrow places? Can I imagine living largely from a small space?

Today's reading is a transition point in the Gospel of Mark. For the first time Christ speaks plainly to his disciples about the coming narrow places of his journey and theirs. Suffering, rejection, death, the cross, losing one's life. Yet, he does not speak of them as places where life is lost but, instead, as opportunities for true life to be found. He invites us to live largely from the narrow spaces of life.

Blessed Jesus, where the spaces of our lives are narrow,
grant us grace to look beyond our limited imaginations,
focusing toward your expanding interests,
opening ourselves to new life. Amen.

JANET DAVIS holds a degree in nursing and a master's in spiritual nurture. Currently working as a hospital chaplain, she loves to garden, travel, and engage in long, lively dinner table conversations with her husband and three teenage children.

Friday of Lent V
Psalm 41

Blessed is anyone who cares for the poor and the weak; in
time of trouble Yahweh rescues [her].

Psalm 41:1

They met during the blackest time of her life, after she had lost a bitter custody fight over her son. Sherri, an RN in a community hospital, wondered how she could contain her emotions and keep her focus on patients during this emotionally difficult time. Mary, her new manager, knew right away what she needed. "I didn't think I could get up in the morning," says Sherri. "Mary made up reasons for me to get out of bed—making copies, putting together packages—a lot of little things for me to do until I was able to function again. And every day for two years, she would come to wherever in the hospital I was working and relieve me so I could go to school and have lunch with my son. I can't tell you how much she has helped me to grow."

This is a true story—one that touches my heart and makes me realize the special connection that can happen between women. In the lectionary readings, several verses draw our attention to caring for the poor and weak. Often we think about giving money to the Star of Hope Mission or giving food offerings for the community Food Bank in our neighborhoods. But what about the poor and weak who live and work and have their being in our midst every day? Perhaps they are not financially poor but, instead, poor in spirit—depressed, depleted, hurting; needing a special touch, understanding, compassion.

"Blessed is anyone who cares for the poor and the weak." We, as women, each have memories of the "Marys" in our individual lives who helped us to get up in the mornings. During this Lenten season, think of the women who have given you courage and have allowed you to "borrow their faith" for a while. And remember the people that your life has touched in life-changing ways. The poor will always be among us, yes. But they don't have to suffer alone.

Spirit of compassion, in the whirlwind of our daily lives,
help us not to miss the opportunities to reach out to others.
Give us wisdom, intuition, and strong boundaries that we might find
the balance of caring for others and caring for ourselves. Amen.

+ PAMELA L. TAYLOR is currently a hospital chaplain. Over the past twenty-five years of ministry, she has also served as a youth minister, college campus minister, and hospice chaplain.

Saturday of Lent V
Genesis 49:1–28

> *Blessings of the breasts and of the womb . . .*
> *Genesis 49:25*

I would remind and remind her—tonight at seven! In the gym! Don't forget! And afterwards, I would drive myself home to see the beautiful new shirt/dress/jacket hanging on my bedroom door. In the inimitable way of a teenager it was high drama: I didn't like it, I wouldn't wear it, it didn't make up for her not being there, I was the only one whose dad was there instead of her mother . . . and then the grand finale as I slammed the door, locking myself in with my hurt, my disappointment, and my oh-so-righteous anger.

The blessings of the breasts and womb—the ability to create and nurture others—is a delicate and dangerous thing. It is a godlike power to produce this new being, and there is such phenomenal tension in caring for another while still taking care of yourself. When I was sixteen it was difficult for me to see that I had a father who was more of a "mother" and a mother who was in the father role. My mother should be watching me dance at halftime, helping me get ready for homecoming, and telling me all the womanly secrets I was sure I was missing! My mother taught me none of that, yet she nurtured and gave to me in a way that has taken me time to see. She taught me to be independent; she taught me that women could be strong and purposeful; she taught me that fathers can love and raise children as well as mothers.

The experience with my mother my creator also gives me knowledge about my relationship with God my creator, especially when I look for God and find only the absence of God. I am reminded that in my fixation with the way things should work and be, I often miss the creations that are actually happening in my life and the lives of those around me. My mother has become an icon. She reminds me to look beyond my expectations and to see past the surface to recognize power that appears in unexpected ways and places, power that has the ability to turn the shirt on the bedroom door into a garment of praise.

AIMEE ESTEP is a proud parent and youth minister living in Austin, Texas.

Holy Week

HOLY WEEK

Palm Sunday
Luke 13:10–17

"Should not this woman, a daughter of Abraham, whom
Satan has kept bound for eighteen long years, be set free
on the Sabbath day from what bound her?"

Luke 13:16

This unnamed woman, known and referred to only by her physical condition, is a powerful role model for all women, then and
now, who live in difficult and hostile circumstances. It would be
easy to read this story and focus solely on what Jesus did for this
woman. The important question today is, what did she do for herself?

The crippled woman could have stayed home that day. She was,
after all, forbidden to be present in the synagogue because of her
physical deformity. Her community believed that illness and disabling
conditions were the direct result of an individual's failure to obey
Mosaic law or, in this case, that she had opened herself to the invasion
of demons.

But the demons were not of her making nor present by her invitation. She was bent over by culturally imposed tradition, ignorance,
poverty, inferior status, objectification, powerlessness, fear, and pro-
found grief at the losses she had endured in her lifetime. Despite her
pain, her shame, her fear, she had the courage to risk putting herself in
a position to be blessed.

This woman who could do nothing to lift herself up believed that
God is a God of mercy and love. She trusted God to restore her to
wholeness. She went to the place where she knew she would be in the
presence of that merciful, loving God, incarnate in Jesus Christ. She

went with a faith like Daniel's that said, "I serve a God who is able to save me, but even if he does not, I will still serve him." Jesus recognized her high position as "a daughter of Abraham" because of her irrational belief that God wants all of creation to be free, lifted up, straight and tall, so that we can praise him.

I know this woman. I am this woman. Too often I am bent over by my own demons. Yet, when I am trudging through the valley, on my way to the cross, so burdened that I cannot stand up straight, I too can choose to trust God.

GEORGIA WADE HOUSER is a wife and mother of three adult sons. She struggles incessantly with the promises of the gospel and the realities of life. An American Baptist, she learned of Brigid's Place from her Episcopalian buddies and is extremely grateful for this holy space where women are free to explore spiritual dimensions.

Monday of Holy Week
Psalm 119:49–72

The LORD is my portion; I promise to keep your words . . .
The arrogant smear me with lies, but with my whole heart
I keep your precepts. Their hearts are fat and gross, but I
delight in your law.

Psalm 119:57, 69–70

The psalmist seems to say that it is his constant struggle to live by God's law and precepts, to justify his life in his love of the commandments and the law. He is anxious and worried that he may not be "doing it right," that others do not keep the law as he does, that they may try to ensnare him.

I remember the first and great commandment, to love God with all my heart and soul and mind—and the second, to love my neighbor as myself. This simplifies for me the struggle the psalmist feels to try to figure out what is the law, what is God's expectation, what is enough. It is enough, most days, for me to love God, to experience God as a presence within me, to let myself be loved as a woman made in her image, struggling to know God and to respond to love so freely given that it is a part of my very being. For I know that within myself are many different selves, pulling me in different directions, sometimes creating chaos and tumult within, sometimes doubt and anger and uncertainty. But if Christ incarnate lives within me, all my different selves can be unified in Christ, who is the center of my being.

From love within me, deeply experienced, I can love others who may disagree with me, who may follow a different path, who may see and experience God in a different way. My experience of a loving God fills me to overflowing, so that God is All and in all and part of myself, who feeds and nourishes me. Together we are whole and complete, male and female. All the disparate parts of myself are one in God. God, indeed, is "better to me than thousands of gold and silver pieces." God in Christ is my experience of love incarnate.

Spirit of love, help me to express the hospitality of God
to those who are different from me.
How can I listen with attention unless I first listen to the voices
in my own heart and the unresolved conflicts in my own heart?
How can I love and respect others if I refuse to meet
and listen to the many sides of myself?
Give me grace to have charity toward myself, so I may be able
to listen, love, and be more charitable toward others. Amen.

MARGARET MAXWELL is a retired social work practitioner and teacher, an Episcopalian and a serious student, and a searcher in the field of Jungian analytic psychology. She treasures each day for its new experiences and revelations and the chance to grow more deeply into God and self.

Tuesday of Holy Week
Mark 10:1–16

Truly I say to you, whoever does not receive the kingdom
of God like a child shall not enter it.
                                                    Mark 10:15

How does Jesus mean for us to be "like a child"? Children are not born with the Book of Knowledge; they learn from experience. They are born with the Spirit of the living God within them, pure and unadulterated by what they will later be taught by word and deed. Children are born as Spirit people.

In *Meeting Jesus Again for the First Time*, Marcus Borg writes: "When screens of consciousness momentarily drop away, the experience of Spirit occurs. A Spirit person is one in whom those screens of consciousness are unusually permeable—compared with most of us, who seem to have hardened into rinds of consciousness instead."

I'm reminded of a story that Marcus Borg told at a seminar about a family with a newborn baby. The parents were apprehensive when their three-year-old daughter wanted to be alone with their new son. But a baby monitor was next to the crib, so they agreed to grant the request. The parents listened in the next room as the little girl crept up to the crib. "What is God like? I'm beginning to forget," she said to her brother.

To be like a child, we must find the experience of the Spirit of the living God within and know it as we knew it then—open, full of love, full of trust—before our "rinds" hardened.

In 2 Corinthians 3:3, Paul says, "You show that you are a letter from Christ . . . written not with ink but with the Spirit of the living God, not on tablets of stone but on tablets of human hearts."

Creator God, I pray this day that we are warmed by your spirit in us,
    and that we go forth with that spirit into a hardened world
as your children, to show forth our experience of your love. Amen.

JUDY MOOD, president of Brigid's Place, is a "seeker" who has lived in the Far East, the Middle East, Europe, and Alaska. She currently resides in Houston, Texas, with her husband Rob.

Marcus Borg, *Meeting Jesus Again for the First Time: The Historical Jesus and the Heart of Contemporary Faith* (San Francisco: HarperSanFrancisco, 1994).

Wednesday of Holy Week
Matthew 27:15–26

> *While [Pilate] was sitting on the judgment seat, his wife*
> *sent word to him, "Have nothing to do with that innocent*
> *man, for today I have suffered a great deal because of a*
> *dream about him."*
>
> *Matthew 27:19*

How tempting it is to keep the Jesus story trapped back in history, contained and controlled on the pages of Holy Scripture. How much easier it is to leave the players in the drama in the first century, irrelevant to my life and times. How quickly one can pass over Pilate's wife and her disturbing dream; after all, she gets only one verse in the entire Jesus story!

If I want to bring that story into my own life, I could use Pilate's wife to say, "See how it was for women? Women had no voice, even when they had the truth!" Then, I can wrap my cloak of righteous indignation around me and feel justified in holding on to my contempt for those who will not hear me speak my truth. When I step into that story, however, I am compelled to recognize that Pilate's wife lives in me, just as surely as Pilate does.

I am Pilate's wife when I don't take my way of knowing seriously, when I discount my intuition, and when I doubt or question the guidance that comes in ways that I, daughter of patriarchy, have learned to ignore. I am Pilate's wife when I overvalue rational, logical guidance and ignore that which is Mystery.

I am Pilate's wife when I send someone else to bear the message that has been given to me instead of stepping forward to give it myself, shrinking from my responsibility because it requires me to stand up to the Pilate that is in me.

I am Pilate's wife when I do not step forward boldly and insist that the truth I know be heard and that the Mystery be honored.

Holy Mystery, please give me another chance
to hear and to bear your message.
Embolden me with holy courage so that I can speak
clearly and forcefully so that I might save the
Christ-in-me from the Pilate-in-me who would give
him away in order to please the crowd. Amen.

JEANIE MILEY is a columnist, retreat leader, and speaker. She is the author of *The Spiritual Art of Creative Silence, Becoming Fire,* and *ChristHeart.*

Maundy Thursday
1 Corinthians 10:14–17, 11:27–32
John 17:1–11

Today's commemoration of the Lord's Supper invites us to probe more deeply into two themes of Eucharist: love and unity.

Paul's words to the Corinthians warn us about the necessity of a loving concern for one another as we approach the table, and remind us that sharing the one loaf of Christ deepens our oneness both with Christ and with the others who receive. We need to take these words of Scripture seriously. They challenge us to ask:

What is the level of my concern for others as I receive Eucharist?

Is love growing in me for God/Jesus? Others?

Is there a deepening oneness between me and God/Jesus? Others?

What prevents Eucharist from having its full effect on me? On our congregation?

Do I really desire the effects from Eucharist that Scripture promises?

The gospel helps our response. In this reading from John, we are privy to a conversational prayer between Jesus and the Father. Unlike the prayer in the garden, Jesus does not ask to be relieved of suffering. He asks for glory—for himself, but also for God, the disciples, and for those who have come to believe through them—for us. The tenderness of Jesus' love shown in this high-priestly prayer opens us to Jesus' desire that we come to share the very oneness that he experiences with the Father.

These are the kind of readings that warrant Annie Dillard's remark that we would wear crash helmets to church if we only understood what we were doing.

Eucharist is about love, unity, shalom, the kingdom where loving God and others becomes possible, and unity among humans and with God, an essential. How far our reality is from this! Is Eucharist ineffective? Or are we not yet receptive to the fullness of its message and its implications?

Holy Thursday is a yearly reminder to probe and live its mystery more profoundly.

SISTER MARY DENNISON is a Religious of the Cenacle stationed at the Cenacle Retreat House in Houston, Texas. She directs a program for training spiritual directors.

Good Friday
John 13:36–38

> *"Rabbi," Peter said, "Why can't I follow you now? I will*
> *lay down my life for you!" "Lay down your life for me?"*
> *exclaimed Jesus. "The truth of the matter is, before the*
> *cock crows you'll have disowned me three times!"*
> *John 13:37–38*

As we prepare to receive the bread and the cup in the Eucharist at Bering Memorial United Methodist Church, we sing the haunting, beseeching words of the Agnus Dei: "Jesus, Lamb of God, have mercy on us. Jesus, bearer of our sins, have mercy on us. Jesus, redeemer of the world, give us your peace."

These words remind us of our need of mercy. We are God's beloved, created in God's image; and we are persons who betray, deny, and fail to live Christ's love. As Christian people, we make promises to live as followers of Jesus the Christ; we mean to be faithful. We pray and study and worship; we cook and visit, sharing our gifts that we might be a blessing to others. We often live the love of Christ. But we are not God. We are human beings, part saint, part sinner, totally dependent on God's grace.

Last summer I took a five-week leave for spiritual renewal. Away from my pastoral work at Bering, I moved more deeply into the experience of God's grace. Day by day I was replenished through sleep and swimming and walking and sitting on the deck overlooking the lake. I opened my heart to God's gift of gracious acceptance and renewal. I didn't have to get it "right" to be God's beloved! I didn't have to preach great sermons or give a soft response to complaints. I could rest in God's love and trust God through all the grief and injustice present in today's church. I could even trust God for my own inadequacies and failure to be a Christlike presence.

I returned from leave newly committed to be a grace-filled presence in our church and world. Then one day last week I forgot that my daughter Lindsay's school had early dismissal. She is eight years old and needed to be picked up from school early. Twenty-five years of parenting, and I forget this basic task! God's word of grace came from the father of Lindsay's friend Kathleen, who called to say they could play together while I finished my meetings. I had betrayed my sacred trust, but there was mercy.

With God there is forgiveness. We who sometimes fail miserably are the very ones who also reflect the love of Christ in a needy world. Others may glimpse God's grace in our love. With God there is mercy, more than enough for you and for me.

+ MARILYN MEEKER-WILLIAMS is senior pastor of Bering Memorial United Methodist Church, which is centered in ministries of healing and wholeness and working for peace with justice. By God's grace, the church seeks to support the full participation of all persons in every phase of church life.

Holy Saturday
Psalms 88, 95
Romans 8:1–11

> *Is your love declared in the grave, your faithfulness in*
> *Destruction?*
>
> *Psalm 88:11*

> *And if the Spirit of him who raised Jesus from the dead is*
> *living in you, he who raised Christ from the dead will also*
> *give life to your mortal bodies through his Spirit, who lives*
> *in you.*
>
> *Romans 8:11*

> *Come, let us sing for joy to the* LORD.
>
> *Psalm 95:1a*

A few years ago, I was given an incredible gift of great sadness and joy at the same time. Our second child, Matthew, was born on Good Friday and we anticipated release from the hospital on Saturday, Holy Saturday. On that day, however, the doctors discovered that he had an inoperable heart defect that would end his life within days.

We had anticipated the birth of this child for nine months. We had looked forward to him, our first son, and during his short lifetime, I fully experienced the great joy of holding this child in my arms. However, I also suffered the deep pain of knowing that his death was soon to come. I lived in the contrast of those emotions until the One who had suffered death himself allowed a grave to enter my own life— a grave that serves as a faithful reminder of God's love. Our time with Matthew was glorious and full of life. Yet, from his death I am able to look forward to the time when the Spirit of God will give life to our mortal bodies in the resurrection just as Jesus was resurrected.

Holy Saturday, the day before our grandest celebration in the Christian church, brings out these conflicting emotions for me. Today's readings are laden with the disparity between sorrow and rejoicing. This is a day of sorrow in the church because we commemorate the mourning over Jesus' death, yet we live in the knowledge that tomorrow brings joyous news of his resurrection. Prior to Matthew's presence in my life, it had always been hard for me to imagine the depth of despair of this day while possessing the knowledge of the joy that is to come.

I reflect upon the sadness of Holy Saturday knowing truly that God's love is declared in the grave: the grave that Jesus entered, offering hope for tomorrow and tomorrow and tomorrow.

CAMILLE RODRIQUEZ is an active supporter of and participant in her husband's ministry as an Episcopal priest in Houston, Texas. They have four children for whom Camille has had the privilege to be mother, home educator, and friend.

Easter Day
Matthew 28:1–10
Mark 16:1–8
Luke 24:1–10
John 20:1–10

> *"Who will roll the stone away for us from the entrance to the tomb?"*
>
> *Mark 16:3*

It doesn't matter which gospel I read today. The stone is always mentioned as an obstacle to the tomb. How will I encounter the resurrection of Christ unless the stone is rolled away?

I first encountered the stone as obstacle while reading *The Road to Daybreak* by Henri Nouwen. He tells one story of an intimate Easter Day Eucharist when one participant raised the issue: "We have to keep rolling away the large stones that prevent people from coming out of their graves." I meditated on what it meant for me to come out of my grave and become new again. How is the stone rolled away for me so I can discover my own resurrections? How do I assist others in rolling away the stones that block discovery of their resurrections?

As I write this, my country is at war. I am not satisfied with our response. Surely a peaceful solution is the resurrection hiding behind a huge stone. I desperately want to find a way to roll this stone away because I believe the resurrection of Jesus calls us to a peaceful solution. Like the women going to the tomb, I pray for the removal of this stone.

Our smaller, daily resurrections are not always recognizable. Just as the forty days of Lent give me time to do my interior work of connecting with the Creator, so also the great fifty days of Easter give me time to externalize this work by proclaiming the miracle of Christ's resurrection, which is also my own resurrection. Finding different and creative ways to roll away the stone is the manifestation of the Creator in me discovering my daily resurrections. I am made new by Christ's resurrection.

Seek ways to roll away the stone to proclaim the peace of Christ's resurrection.

Alleluia, Alleluia!
Christ is risen! Christ is risen in me! Christ is risen in the world!
Alleluia, Alleluia!

LUCY WAGNER is a Christian educator and mentor. She is active in developing worship liturgies with the Worship Weavers of Brigid's Place.

Henri J. M. Nouwen, *The Road to Daybreak: A Spiritual Journey* (New York: Image Books, 1990), 163.